A Police Wife Bible Study

Melissa Humes

DEDICATION

May the Lord be glorified.

I love you, Andrew.

THANKS

Many thanks to my daughter Katherine Anne for her help in editing this work.

Thank you to Grace Bible Church for permission to use their Bible Study Methods.

Thank you, Trisha, for the initial encouragement.

Thank you for the many prayer warriors who prayed during this whole process.

CONTENTS

Introduction

INTRODUCTION

Coping and facing law enforcement challenges is crucial. Our law enforcement officers need us and our children need us, but we cannot meet their needs if our life feels hollow, empty, and drained. Each challenge we are confronted with has choices and some of those will lead us down a path that can ultimately destroy us, our marriages, and our children. These challenges will be faced, and we need to work through them to prevent the destructive nature of one of our biggest enemies- bitterness. There is hope in a different way — daily choices leading to the path of joy, contentment, trust, and love. The Bible holds the answers: Jesus fills the emptiness and hollowness of our lives. God's Word breathes life into our dry spirits. When we give our life to Him, He takes our brokenness and turns it into healing and fullness; He equips us to give back to others. This is the only way to walk through the trials of life. This is not an exhaustive list of issues law enforcement wives face, but hopefully you can wrestle with these and be encouraged to search out answers as you learn to study the Bible and apply it to your everyday life.

1 **LONELINESS**

You have been to what seems like the hundredth family event alone. Everyone at some point comes up to you asking where your husband is, and how he is doing, and expresses sympathy that he is not with you . . . again. Birthdays, weddings, funerals, holidays, church, sporting events, school events — the hollow feeling of loneliness during such times can swing from "It's okay, I'm used to this," to "I really can't face another event alone." Loneliness can become a palpable ache. It can also lead to an enemy, bitterness. The baby steps of becoming angry every time you do one of "these things" alone — again — is the path to bitterness. Loneliness while being married is one of the things you are not always prepared for as a LEO wife. You may not have known it was going to be a big deal until years into this police life you found that it doesn't always get better.

This chapter's passage deals with a man of God in Israel who felt lonely.

Read I Kings 19

1. (vs. 1-8) Elijah flees Ahab and Jezebel after defeating Baal and the 450 false Baal prophets on Mt. Carmel (ch. 18). Where does he run to? Why is this significant? (cr. rf. Matt. 4:1-2, Ex. 16:1-21; 31-35.) What is Elijah's state of mind? Who do you think Elijah is focused on at this point? Who sustains Elijah in the wilderness?

2. (vs. 9-14) Elijah comes to Mt. Horeb after 40 days and nights. What is another name for Mt. Horeb? Who else met God on this mountain? (cr. rf. Ex. 19:1-6.) Why do you think Elijah fled to this mountain?

3. Elijah had his eyes on himself and his aloneness. How did God finally reveal Himself to Elijah?

4. (vs. 15-21) After God brings Elijah to a place of revelation, He gives him instructions for his next assignment. What does God point out to Elijah? Who does God give to Elijah to help him?

Application Questions

1. Where/who do you run to when you feel lonely? Who should you focus on when you encounter loneliness? Who sustains you during your loneliness?

2. How does God reveal Himself to you? God's act of revealing Himself to you can draw you out of your loneliness. How can you learn who God is through this process?

3. Who has God brought alongside that can help you and walk with you?

Memory Verse: Joshua 1:9 "Have I not commanded you? Be strong and courageous! Do not tremble or be dismayed, **for the Lord your God is with you wherever you go**."

Song for Encouragement: "Never Once" by Matt Redman

Key Helpful Points:

- When faced with loneliness, run to God and listen to His voice.

- Meditate on His Word, His truths, His promises.

- Tell God your anger at being lonely and let Him take it from you.

- Take your eyes from your loneliness, turn your eyes to God, and look at what He has done for you.

- Pray for God to bring you a friend who can help you through the tough times.

- Seek encouragement from other LEO wives through books, fellowship, and conferences.

2 **FEAR**

His shift ended at two am. You look blearily at the clock and realize it is five am. You check your phone—no messages. Fear grips your heart. You are now wide awake. You text him, hoping for an immediate response. It doesn't come—more fear. Then finally, "I'm okay, got tied up with a DWI right before shift ended but headed home soon." We all know the relief when we hear the Velcro being pulled from that bullet proof vest. It doesn't matter what time of day or night we hear it, that sound means he is home and safe. There are too many stories of law enforcement officers who never come home. Fear of being the one with a knock at your door in the middle of the night. Fear of him getting hurt so badly he can't work anymore. Living with that kind of fear can either paralyze us or keep us on our knees. Sometimes dealing with constant fear can turn us against the very person we are worried about because we are resentful that fear is a part of our lives.

Scripture is filled with imperfect, real people. This chapter's

passage speaks of a very fearful servant.

Read 2 Kings 6:8-23

1. (vs. 8-12) King Ben-Hadad of Aram was annoyed that his

   surprise raids on Israel kept becoming known. What was

   he told about how this was happening?

2. (vs. 13-14) Did Ben-Hadad seem to believe in the

   supernatural working through Elisha?

3. (vs.15) What was Elisha's servant's reaction to the

    Aramean army surrounding Elisha and he with horses and

    chariots?

4. (vs.16-17) What was Elisha's answer to his servant's great

    fear? Why was Elisha not afraid? (cr. rf. 2 Kings 2:12, 1

    Chron. 21:15-16, Ps. 34:7).

5. One man, Elisha, led the blinded Aramean army into the heart of enemy territory, Israel's capital city, Samaria. What happened to them once they were captured? (In ancient times eating a meal together was a peace-covenant, so they were bound by custom not to attack the friend who had extended hospitality.)

Application Questions

1. What is your initial reaction when you are facing unknown circumstances?

2. Do you trust and believe in God's sovereign power over everything? How can you remind yourself of this when you are fearful?

3. If fear has gripped you, reading, mediating on, and memorizing His truths can help face those fears. Here are some additional verses: Ps. 27:1, Isa. 41:10 & 13, Prov. 3:24-26, Isa. 42:6, Isa. 43:1-3

Memory Verse: Isaiah 41:10, "**Do not fear**, for I am with you; do not anxiously look about you, for I am your God. I will strengthen you, surely I will help you, surely I will uphold you with My righteous right hand."

Song for Encouragement: "Whom Shall I Fear" by Chris Tomlin

Key Helpful Points:

- God is sovereign.
- There is an unseen army of angels ready to do God's bidding.

- Memorize and mediate on Scripture that focuses on facing fears, overcoming fear, giving fear to God, etc.

- Trust that God has you and your loved ones in His hands no matter what happens.

- Share your fears with a friend who can pray with you and encourage you.

3 **HARASSMENT**

At the mildest, you are subjected to hearing everyone complaining about their most recent ticket. You remind your children not to tell strangers what their dad does for a living. You are sometimes afraid to wear your police-wife gear outside of the house. There are restaurants at which your family cannot eat because of staff hostility towards law enforcement. Vile language is thrown in your face at the mention of your husband's occupation. Your husband writes reports because criminals have verbally threatened his family. The word "PIG" is spray-painted on your house. You watch the violence and hatred aimed at law enforcement around the country on television. How do you support him and protect your children without falling into the same cycle of anger and bitterness?

The Apostle Paul was also harassed and maligned for standing up to corruption and wrongdoing.

Read Acts 16:16-34

1. (vs. 16-18) Paul and Silas went to Phillippi, an important city in the district of Macedonia, a Roman colony. Who was bothering them as they tried to go about their business? What did Paul finally do about it?

    a. Why do you think Paul did not want this truth of the gospel proclaimed through a demon? (cr. rf. Luke 8:27-30).

2. (vs. 19-24) The slave girl's masters were furious because "their hope of profit was gone". What did they do to Paul and Silas?

3. (vs. 25-29) What were Paul and Silas doing while in prison? What emotions do you think they were experiencing? What does God do? (cr. rf. Ps. 42).

4. (vs.30-34) What happened because of Paul's and Silas's

   actions?

Application Questions

1. How do you react when your husband or your family is harassed?

2. Paul immediately knew the root source of the harassment. How can this knowledge help with some of the hatred and violence we see and experience?

3. Based on what Paul and Silas were doing at midnight in the prison, what is a proper reaction to adversity?

Memory Verse: James 1:2, "**Consider it all joy**, my brethren, when you encounter various trials, knowing that the testing of your faith produces endurance."

Song for Encouragement: "O' Lord" by Lauren Daigle

Key Helpful Points:

- Recognize where hatred and violence really come from: Satan.

- God can use any situation to further the gospel and bring others to Him.

- Despite being wronged or harassed, look to Jesus, and *praise Him.*

- Joy comes when our eyes are on Jesus and not on ourselves or our situation.

4 DEPRESSION

There is a heavy, dark blanket that envelopes and smothers a person. It is the feeling of dread that this LEO life will never get better. That it will never end. Are we counting down the days until he retires? Then, we think, we can start living life again. Sometimes it feels impossible to face years of this job taking a toll on us and our children. It is even worse when we see signs of this weighing on our husbands: the things he has seen, the things he must live with, the nightmares. When he sits in his chair at home and weeps for the trauma he has witnessed and experienced. Too many officers die at their own hands. The feelings of *worthlessness, helplessness, and then hopelessness* lead to suicide. There is a stigma that makes us think that if I show this deep, dark despair, "I am weak." How do we fight this black cloud that descends so indiscriminately?

Job knew despair, trauma, and helplessness like few who have ever lived.

Read Job 1 and 2; 10:1-2, 18-22; 38, 39, and 42

1. (ch. 1:1-13) Describe Job's life, his standing with God, and Satan's taunt.

2. (ch. 1:13-22) Describe what happened to Job and his reaction to his circumstances.

3. (ch. 2) Describe what further happens to Job and his reaction to these events.

4. (ch. 10:1-2, 18-22) Write down some of the words Job uses to express his feelings.

5. (ch. 8 and 39) After Job's friends spend chapters wrongly accusing Job and misinterpreting God's actions, God speaks. What is God trying to say to Job through these powerful examples?

6. (ch. 42) What is Job's attitude towards God after all this? How does God end Job's story?

Application Questions

1. How do your life circumstances effect your view of God?

2. How does your view of God change the way you look at your present circumstances?

3. If God's power and might can do the things He claims in chapters 38 and 39, do you think He has power over your circumstances?

Memory Verse: Psalm 40:1-3, "I waited patiently for the Lord; and He inclined to me and heard my cry. He brought me up out of the pit of destruction, out of the miry clay; and He set my feet upon a rock making my footsteps firm. And He put a new song in my mouth, a song of praise to our God; many will see and fear and will trust in the Lord."

Song for Encouragement: "Oceans" by Hillsong United

Key Helpful Points:

- Acknowledging God's sovereign control and His mighty power over all creation keeps our life anchored to Him.

- Trust in the Lord in all your circumstances.

- Practice praising and thanking God every day (write a list of all you are thankful for).

- Talk about what has happened to you and what is going on with people you trust.

- Seek professional counselors and help when things seem hopeless (see Appendix C for resources).

5 **FATIGUE**

Frustration can boil over when we see him sitting in his chair, staring at his phone or the television in what seems like a weekly off-day pattern. Sometimes he has a hard time concentrating and questions of any caliber can be difficult for him to process. There is a lack of focus; they seem to be listening, but they are not "hearing" or engaging in the conversation. They can be too tired to do anything productive. Much of this is a symptom of continual hypervigilance and the roller coaster hormonal biological effects. The long-lasting adrenaline surges, the quickly falling depletion of those hormones, and the leveling back to normal is a daily cycle that if not recognized can result in irrevocable relationship damage.

Solomon was the third king of Israel and the son of King David by

Bathsheba. His reign was one of the richest, wisest, and most

peaceful in the history of Israel. At the end of his rule, he wrote

the book of Ecclesiastes as a summary of his life's observations.

Read Ecclesiastes 3:1-14

1. What is the thesis statement of the passage as stated in

   verse 1?

2. Verses 2-8 comprises a list of opposites. From this list,

   which ones can you not control? Which ones do you

   control?

3. In verse 9, Solomon asks if man knows the value or the why of his works/labors. Verse 10 responds. Who gives man his tasks in life?

4. Complete the sentence: He has made everything

_____ in its time. Look up the Hebrew word and list the meanings. (www.biblestudytools.com)

5. Complete the sentence: God has set _____ in the hearts of men. Look up the Hebrew word and list the meanings. (www.biblestudytools.com)

6. Paraphrase verse 13 in your own words.

Application Questions

1. Can having an eternal perspective change your motivation for your work in life?

2. Can the promise that God makes all things beautiful in its time give you peace in your present circumstances?

3. We shouldn't let one thing control all our time because everything has a place. How do you balance your time and not let one thing overwhelm all life?

4. What is something you can do to help normalize the hypervigilant cycle in your spouse this week?

5. Set aside a time during "normal" cycle levels to get a game plan together with your spouse in relation to exercise, the calendar, recreational activities, eating habits, and limits to "sitting" time.

Memory Verse: Ecclesiastes 4:9-10

Song for Encouragement: "Turn! Turn! Turn!" by The Byrds

Key Helpful Points:

- Realize that there is a 18-24-hour recovery period for normalizing the hypervigilant cycle.

- Aerobic exercise for 30-40 minutes 4-5 times a week (especially directly after the end of a shift) can help normalize adrenal levels faster.

- Schedule off time beforehand during normal levels and stick to the family calendar as best as possible. Planning avoids indecision and complacency.

- Prioritize doing non-police related activities on off days, things you enjoy doing together.

- Eat regular and healthy (packing healthy premade frozen meals for work can greatly decrease the eating-out habit).

6 JEALOUSY

Your husband's new partner is a young female rookie. You fight feelings of jealousy even if you trust your husband completely. Extra training days and meetings, travel, so much time spent with squad mates: 12-14-hour days with them compared to the 30 minutes to an hour you may get on those days. Promotions or assignments can pass over your husband, going to others. We get jealous of THE JOB with all the demands it places on him and how it can take him away from us. Jealousy creeps into our hearts in so many ways. Jealousy, when allowed to take root, has a serious and frightening consequence, one that should stop us in our tracks.

Let's look at several situations in Scripture where jealousy fueled decisions and then look at their outcomes.

Read Genesis 4:1-15: Cain and Abel

1.   What was Cain jealous about?

2.   What was the outcome of his unchecked jealousy?

Read 1 Samuel 18:5-16: Saul and David

1.   What was the reason for Saul's jealousy towards David? (cr. rf. Prov. 6:34, Prov. 27:4).

2. What did Saul's jealousy eventually lead him to do? (cr. rf.
1 Sam. 19:8-10).

Read Matthew 2:1-18: Herod and Jesus

1. What "troubled" Herod?

2. What did Herod's enraging jealousy cause him to do?

3. Look up some historical facts on Herod and note a pattern
of behavior. (www.biblestudytools.com)

Read Mark 2-3:6, 8:1-13, 11:27-12:12, 14:1-2, and 14:10-11:

Pharisees and Jesus

1. The Pharisees had become increasingly irritated and

   jealous of Jesus' massive followings. How is this evident?

2. What did the Pharisees finally do about Jesus? (cr. rf. John

   18-19:30).

Application Questions

1. Based on the examples from Scripture, where does

   jealousy end? Does this frighten you?

2. How should this outcome effect your initial dabbling in

   jealous thoughts? How can you use this to check your

   emotions?

3. Read Philippians 1:12-20. The Apostle Paul could have fallen into jealousy when other people were enviously trying to preach the gospel, causing Paul distress. What was Paul's response, and how should this be my response? (cr. rf. Romans 13:13-14; What is the command in verse 14?).

4. Read James 3:16-18. Wisdom is contrasted with jealousy and strife. What two things are born of jealousy (vs. 16)? Wisdom replaces jealousy with what attributes (vs.17)?

Memory Verse: James 3:16-17, "For where jealousy and selfish ambition exist, there is disorder and ever evil thing. But the wisdom from above is first pure, then peaceable, gentle, reasonable, full of mercy and good fruits, unwavering without hypocrisy."

Song for Encouragement: "In Christ Alone" by Keith Getty and Stuart Townend

Key Helpful Points:

- Be aware of jealousy's consequences.
- Don't "chew on" or ruminate on jealous thoughts. It is like playing with fire.
- Based on James 3:16-18, seek wisdom in your life situations, knowing that true wisdom from above looks like the wisdom in James 3:17.
- Seek the Lord's will in all circumstances. Seek Christ proclaimed and exalted through your behavior (Phil. 1:18-20).

- Rest in the knowledge that in Christ alone your worth

  stands. He is your all in all through all.

7 **INTEGRITY**

Integrity: "The entire, unimpaired state of anything, particularly of the mind. Moral soundness or purity, incorruptness, uprightness, honesty" (Noah Webster's *1828 Dictionary*).

We hope integrity in law enforcement is a given; it is the foundation on which justice rests. Integrity weaves itself into all areas of our lives; even in little decisions that ultimately lead to larger outcomes. Integrity matters most when we are alone, when no one is looking, when we think it matters least. Little choices, little things. Law enforcement officers and their wives need to be wise and follow the path of integrity.

Read Psalms 15:1-2, 25:21, 26:1 & 11, Proverbs 2:6-8, 10:9, 11:3, 19:1, 20:7, 28:6

1. What are the attributes/actions of those with integrity?

2. What are some promises listed in these verses made to those who walk in integrity?

3. Look up the Hebrew word for integrity in a Bible concordance and write its definition.

4. What is the significance of the high priest's breast piece being in the Hebrew definition of integrity? What is the definition of the words Urim and Thummin? (cr. rf. Exodus 28:29-30).

Application Questions

1. Look at your list of attributes and actions from question 1. Which ones do you have the most trouble enacting?

2. How can the promises from this passage towards those with integrity help you to make wise decisions during times of pressure?

Memory Verse: Psalm 15:1-2, "O Lord, who may abide in Thy tent? Who may dwell on Thy holy hill? He who walks with integrity, and works righteousness, and speaks truth in his heart."

Song for Encouragement: "Slow Fade" by Casting Crowns

Helpful Tips:

- Let every decision you make, no matter how small, show integrity, no matter how difficult.

- Remember God's promises for those with integrity.

- Rely on the Holy Spirit to strengthen and guide your heart in making wise judgements in life, standing before the Lord continually.

8 **MARRIAGE**

He is your hero. You see him like no one else does—his ups, his downs. You know what he goes through only by what you see when he comes home. You have endured crazy schedules, including being extremely flexible for times of intimacy. Your heart walks out the door when he puts on that uniform and goes to work. Our marriages bear the brunt of this law enforcement life. Sometimes it is near impossible to find time to be together—it takes a lot of extra effort. The divorce rate in law enforcement is not good. How do we keep our marriages from contributing to this statistic? God's prescription for love can resolve the toughest problems that a marriage can face.

Read 1 Corinthians 13

1. Verses 1-3 describe some actions that without love are described as what?

2. Use an English dictionary to locate the definition of these positive-action words and write them down, then find the Greek word used in the passage and its definition. In the third column, write what action you should take based on these definitions. (www.biblestudytools.com)

English	**Greek**	**Action to Take**

Patient-

Kind-

Truth-

Bears-

Believes-

Hopes-

Endures-

3. Now do the same thing for the negative action words in the passage.

English	Greek	Action to Take

Jealous-

Brag-

Proud-

Selfish-

Rude-

Angry-

Longsuffering-

Unrighteousness-

Application Questions

1. When faced with difficulties in your marriage what are your most common reactions? How does this line up with 1 Cor. 13?

2. "Perfect practice makes perfect." Use this next week to change one of your bad habit reactions. Every time you choose the 1 Cor. 13 reaction, you are one step closer to making it a good life habit. Write about your progress below.

Memory Verse: 1 Corinthians 13:4-8a

Song for Encouragement: "The Proof of Your Love" by For King and Country

Key Helpful Points:

- Pray daily for your spouse and with your spouse for your marriage.

- Commit to do something together every year that focuses on your marriage – a book, Bible study, weekend conference, counseling, etc.

- Practice the actions of 1 Cor. 13 daily.

- Find a mentor couple who can come alongside you and your spouse and encourage your marriage.

- Set aside a weekly date to spend time together and talk.

9 "SINGLE" PARENTING

Our husbands are not exactly available when they are working.
We can text them, and we may get a response hours later, though
sometimes not until the next day. Teenagers need direction,
guidance, and a "life coach," with melt downs and drama
happening at the oddest hours. College kids call us with major life
stresses and need advice and counsel transitioning to adulthood.
The eleven-year-old needs ball practice, so out we go in the
backyard, doing our best. There are late night homework
dilemmas. A young child has medical problems that need
research, decisions, and endless appointments. How many
emergency room visits can we negotiate alone with multiple kids
in tow? We discipline the young ones, needing guidance
constantly. Siblings need an impartial "judge" way too often.
Babies need us ALL THE TIME. We are drained, exhausted. Why
does it feel like we are single parenting while married? We didn't
sign up for this, so we go down that path, getting angry and bitter.

There was once a widow in Israel who learned of God's
faithfulness.

Read 2 Kings 4:1-7. Widows were especially vulnerable in ancient
times, and this story shows God's concern for women.

1. (vs. 1) What was the widow's problem, and who did she
   go to for help? (cr. rf. Exodus 22:22 & 23).

2. (vs.2-3) What does Elisha tell the widow to do?

3. (vs. 5-6) What happened when the widow obeyed?

4. (vs. 7) What was the result of this miracle? (cr. rf. Ps. 68:5).

Application Questions

1. Who/what do you go to when you are at the proverbial "end of the rope" concerning children? What is your reaction to them when you reach this point?

2. The number of jars the widow collected shows her great faith. All the jars collected were filled; you can feel like you have a room full of empty vessels in your heart, but are you willing to give as many as you can to the Lord for Him to fill?

3. This story (and the one following in the chapter) show God's tender concern and care for women. How many times do you fall on your knees to ask God for help with your children and parenting?

Memory verse: Psalm 23

Song for Encouragement: "God, I Look to You" by Francesca Battistelli

Key Helpful Points:

- God's grace is never ending and abundant and, in faith, we can always come to Him with our empty vessels to fill.

- Turn your eyes to Jesus when you don't know what to do or what to say to your children and then listen for His voice.

- God truly cares for women, especially those who are alone; let Him be a father to your children.

- Just as Elisha was used by God to help the widow, let other godly people in your life help fill in the gaps (grandparents, family members, teachers, youth leaders, pastors).

10 **Resentment**

"I *hate* this job!" Angry tears flowed down my face as he walked out the door. He was required to be on duty for an emergency diplomatic situation on the days we were planning to go on a special trip out of town. An extremely rare weekend away at a fancy hotel, seeing our daughter's last college concert. The only concert in three years he would have been able to attend. His assignment has him working 52 weekends a year. Every weekend off is precious vacation time taken. We could not afford elaborate excursions or fancy hotels — this trip was a rare exception. Now I was looking at doing it alone. Waves of feeling sorry for myself, for the hurt and disappointment it would cause our daughter, and anger kept crashing over me. Resentment was building quickly inside of me. I knew this was an internal struggle. Winning this battle was crucial — every incident where resentment won and sunk deep into my soul was another weight added in Satan's pursuit to sink my marriage. Resentment and bitterness are mortal enemies of relationships. How do we fight this battle?

Read Ephesians 6:10-18 (Hint: read this passage in several different translations.)

1. The word "strong" is *endunamoo* in Greek, meaning "to empower, grow strong, increase in strength." Where does our strength lie? (vs.10)

2. List all the entities that are mentioned as our enemies. Also note where their jurisdiction lies. (vs.11-13)

3. The "armor of God" has six components that help us stand and withstand the enemy.

   Belt: What does a belt do? What is the 'belt' in our life, according to verse 14?

   Breastplate: What does a breastplate protect? What offers this protection as stated in verse 14?

   Foot Wear: What does foot wear offer to our feet? What gives us this in verse 15?

Shield: What does the shield protect us from?

What is the 'shield' based on verse 16?

Helmet: The helmet offers protection to what,

metaphorically? What gives us boldness to

withstand the enemies' attacks in the form of the

'helmet' in verse 17?

Sword- The sword is the only offensive weapon in this list. To combat the enemy's assaults and make him flee, what is used in verse 17? (cr. rf. John 4:1-11) How does Jesus resist Satan in the desert according to John?

Application Questions

1. Knowing you have an enemy and that he is using his
    tactics to destroy you is one of the first steps in fighting
    this spiritual battle. List some areas where you feel
    vulnerable and Satan uses to attack you and your
    marriage/family.

2. "Putting on" the armor of God in our lives means to make

   them an integral part of; the Greek word used here, *enduo*

   means "to clothe, be clothed with, dressed, enter, put on,

   in a sense of sinking into a garment." What specific actions

   do you need to take to implement the essential spiritual

   disciplines described?

3. When anger, resentment, and bitterness start to invade your spirit, recognizing it early on is crucial. What should your first action be when you see symptoms of these (cr. rf. James 4:7, 1 Peter 5:6-10).

4. Ephesians 6:18 has the way in which a Christian is to take up the armor of God. What verbs are used here? *How* are these actions to be done?

Memory Verse: James 4:7, "Submit therefore to God. Resist the devil and he will flee from you. Draw near to God and He will draw near to you."

Song for Encouragement: "Head to Toe (The Armor of God song)" by Christy Nockels

Key Helpful Points:

- Recognize and remember who the real enemy in our life is: Satan.

- Lean on the Lord for His strength in seemingly impossible situations.

- Evaluate each part of the armor of God and determine where you stand in putting on each of them.

- As anger, resentment, and bitterness rear their ugly heads, "pray at all times" and "be on the alert." Do these "in the Spirit" and "with all perseverance."

- Go to a quiet, private place to pray as you petition the Lord: a closet, somewhere outdoors, in the car.

- Enlist fellow believers in praying with you and for you.

We are not fighting this battle alone.

Appendix A

How to Know God

God loves you and has a plan for YOU.

The Bible says, "God so loved the world that He gave His one and only Son, (Jesus Christ), that whoever believes in Him shall not perish, but have eternal life" (John 3:16).

Jesus said, "I have come that they may have life and have it abundantly" (John 10:10).

But there is a problem: man is sinful and separated from God.

We have all sinned: thought or done bad things, which the Bible calls "sin."

"For all have sinned and fall short of the glory of God" (Romans 3:23).

"For whoever keeps the whole law and yet stumbles at just one point is guilty of breaking all of it" (James 2:10).

The result of sin is death- spiritual separation from God.

"For the wages of sin is death..." (Romans 6:23.)

The good news: God sent His Son to die for your sins.

Jesus died in our place so we could have a relationship with God and be with Him forever.

"God demonstrates His own love towards us, in that while we were yet sinners, Christ died for us" (Romans 5:8).

The story did not end on the cross, though. Jesus Christ rose again on the third day, defeating death, and lives! "Christ died for our sins according to the Scriptures. That He was buried, that He was raised on the third day, according to the Scriptures" (1 Corinthians 15:3-4).

Jesus is the only way to restore the broken relationship with God. Jesus said, "I am the way, the truth, the life; no one comes to the Father but through Me" (John 14:6).

"The Father has sent His Son to be the Savior of the world" (1 John 4:14).

You can receive God's forgiveness.

We can't earn salvation; we are saved by God's grace when we have faith in His Son, Jesus Christ, as the one who died for our sins, to take the guilt away.

"For by grace are you saved through faith, and not of yourselves, it is the gift of God, lest anyone should boast" (Ephesians 2:8-9).

Believing that you are a sinner, that Jesus Christ died for your sin, turning from your sin (repentance), and asking for His forgiveness brings God's forgiveness into your life and repairs that broken relationship.

"Believe in the Lord Jesus Christ, and you will be saved" (Acts 16:31).

"Therefore, having been justified by faith we have peace with God through our Lord Jesus Christ" (Romans 5:1).

Confess your sin to God and tell Him you believe in His Son Jesus Christ.

"If we confess our sins, He is faithful and just to forgive us our sins and cleanse us from all unrighteousness" (1 John 1:9).

"I am not ashamed of the gospel, because it is the power of God for the salvation of everyone who believes." (Romans 1:16)

You can pray a prayer like this or just tell God in your own words: "Dear God, I know I am a sinner and I ask for your forgiveness. I believe Jesus Christ is Your Son. I believe that He died for my sin and rose again. I want to trust Him as my savior and follow Him as my Lord. Guide my life and help me to do Your will. I pray this in Jesus' Name, Amen."

Appendix B

How to Get the Most

Out of Studying

Your Bible

Observe: What do I see?

Every time we study the Bible, the first thing to ask is, "What do I see?" This is the crucial skill of observation, and it lays the groundwork for the rest of our study.

Here are four tasks involved in observation which should be performed in the order below:

Observation Task 1: Mark up the passage by visually identifying the following elements:

• **Underline all verbs.** A verb is a word or group of words used to indicate either that an action takes place ("I thank my God") or that a state or condition exists ("God is faithful"). Verbs are often the most significant indicators of the author's flow of thought.

• **Circle key words or phrases.** These are words or short phrases that are important theologically (like "word of the cross" in 1:18) or thematically (they set the theme or main idea for the passage, such as "wisdom" and "foolishness" in 1:18-31).

• **Highlight repeated words or phrases.** Include words and phrases that are closely related even if not exact duplicates (such as "judgment" and "judging"). You'll want to highlight things that are repeated from previous passages (such as "Now concerning" found in 7:1, 25; 8:1; 12:1; 16:1).

• **Box connecting words.** These important words indicate the logical connection between words, phrases, and clauses. Here are eight types of common connecting words to look for:

1. **COMPARISON:** either points out similarities between two or more related ideas or simply joins like ideas. Comparison words include: **and, like, as, just as, also, so also, even so** (e.g. "LIKE a wise master builder I laid a foundation" 3:10).

2. CONTRAST: points out dissimilarities between ideas. Contrast words include: **but, rather, yet, however** (e.g. "Jews ask for signs ... BUT we preach Christ crucified" 2:22-23).

3. PURPOSE: indicates the intended goal of an idea or action. Purpose words include: **that, so that, in order that** (e.g. ""I have made myself a slave to all THAT I might win the more" 9:19).

4. RESULT: very similar to "purpose," but indicates the actual consequence, whether it was intended. Result words include: **that, so that, as a result, with the result that** (e.g. "I baptized none of you except Crispus and Gaius SO THAT no one would say . . ." 1:14-15).

5. CAUSE: expresses the basis or cause of an action. Cause words include: **because, since and sometimes for** (e.g. "I praise you BECAUSE you remember me in everything" 11:2).

6. EXPLANATION: what follows further explains the previous idea, giving reasons as to why it is true or why it

occurred or simply adding additional information. Look for the
key word **for**

(e.g. "FOR by one Spirit we were all baptized into one body"
12:13).

7. INFERENCE: provides a logical consequence, a
conclusion, or a summary to the previous discussion. Inference
words include: **therefore, for this reason** (e.g."FOR THIS
REASON, I have sent to you Timothy" 4:17).

8. CONDITION: presents a condition that must occur
before a certain action or conclusion can occur. The statement may
or may not reflect reality (i.e. it could be hypothetical). Key word
is **if** (e.g. "IF any man's work which he has built on it remains, he
will receive a reward" 3:14).

Observation Task 2: List 2-3 primary themes you see in the
passage each week. A primary theme is the big idea, the central
truth or command that the passage focuses on, such as "the
wisdom of God" and "the Spirit reveals truth" in 1:18-2:16. After

reading the passage, write your themes as single words or short phrases. Identifying these themes at the beginning of your study will help you develop a good overall grasp of the passage.

Observation Task 3: Write two or more observations per verse. Oservations might identify people, places, or events, point out repeated words or key terms, record important connections between words and sentences, or even point out something missing that we expected to see.

Observation Task 4: Record your own interpretive questions. Here are a few examples:

WHAT is the...

. . . meaning of this word?

. . . significance of this phrase?

. . . implication of this statement?

. . . relationship between these phrases?

WHY did Paul . . .

. . . choose this word?

. . . include this phrase, statement,

or command?

. . . connect these ideas?

. . . not say _____?

WHO is . . .

. . . Paul talking about?

. . . accomplishing the action?

. . . benefiting from it?

How …

… was this action accomplished?

… will this situation occur?

Interpret: What does it mean?

Our observation of a passage should have stirred up interesting yet challenging questions, leading us to the second stage of our Bible study: interpretation. Fortunately, we do not have to run to a commentary or study Bible for answers (though these are helpful tools to check our conclusions). Use the following six methods, as needed, to tackle a variety of questions, and make sure to familiarize yourself with the three "Principles of Interpretation" below:

<u>**Principle #1**</u> - Your goal is to discern the author's intended meaning to the original audience. Unfortunately, most people begin their Bible study by asking, "What does this passage mean to me?" While there may be multiple possible applications to my life, there is only one meaning, the author's intended meaning; and we must first seek this out. This involves three important steps:

1. Always start your study with prayer, asking the same God who composed Scripture through these ancient authors to give insight to understand His intended meaning.

2. Be very careful to avoid reading your twenty first century circumstances and theological issues into the text as they will skew our understanding.

3. Work diligently to see the text from the point of view of the original readers. To do this: a) dig into the historical and cultural background using Bible dictionaries and commentaries, and b) spend a few moments thinking about the original audience's religious understanding by asking — What books of the Bible did they have access to? What did they know about God? about Jesus? About salvation?

Principle #2 - Assume a normal use of language. The Bible was given to us because God desires to communicate with us, not to hide Himself from us. Therefore, we should not be looking for "hidden" meanings as we study. Instead, we should use the "normal" techniques we would use to understand any piece of literature:

1. Study the grammar. Yes, most of us hated grammar in junior high, but it really is helpful for understanding Scripture! Pay attention to nouns, verbs, adjectives, and prepositions. Think through any figures of speech. Observe how phrases and clauses are connected into sentences and how sentences are linked together into paragraphs.

2. Remember that chapters came later. When Paul wrote Corinthians or Luke wrote the book of Acts, they wrote single, unified stories without verse or chapter divisions. These books were meant to be read just like you would read a letter or a novel. Always keep the overall story in mind as you study each passage.

Principle #3 - **Let Scripture interpret Scripture.** Since God is unchangingly truthful and always consistent (Jn. 7:17; Heb. 3:6; Jam. 1:17), we can, and should, expect the same of His word. This has two practical applications:

1.Check your conclusions. Always compare your conclusions with the teachings of Scripture. If you find that your interpretation of a passage contradicts the clear teaching of Scripture elsewhere, you probably need to revise your conclusions.

2. Allow clear passages to illuminate ambiguous passages. Whenever you encounter a passage that is confusing or open to multiple possible interpretations, use clearer passages of Scripture to guide you to the correct interpretation. One last caution - remember that God revealed Scripture progressively, not all at once. Therefore, we should not be surprised by differences between how people related to and understood God at different times in the history of Scripture. For example, while Abraham needed to only believe that God was faithful in order to be justified (Gen. 15:6), in the New Testament era, we must believe in the death, burial, and resurrection of Jesus to be saved (1 Cor. 15:1-7).

Interpretive Method 1: Use the context. Look for important clues in the sentences and paragraphs that come before and after the verse in question. Try to follow Paul's flow of thought through the whole chapter. This may take you to the previous lesson, so have it handy as a review. You may need to read ahead in 1 Corinthians for clues.

Interpretive Method 2: Compare multiple translations. You can often find helpful interpretive clues by comparing this translation with other translations. The New King James Version (NKJV) and the New American Standard Bible (NASB) are word-for-word translations of the Greek text. The New International Version (NIV) and the New Revised Standard Version (NRSV) are excellent phrase-to-phrase translations of the Greek and are thus often easier to read. Another excellent phrase-to-phrase Bible, which includes extensive translation notes is the New English Translation (NET) available online for free at www.bible.org. You can find and compare numerous translations of any Bible passage at www.biblestudytools.net.

Interpretive Method 3: Look up key words. While looking up a key word in English is helpful, doing so in Greek is far better and is surprisingly easy thanks to the internet. Simply log onto www.biblestudytools.net, and as an example, type in "1 Cor. 2" in

the search for: box, set the "using:" box "to NAS with Strong's

Numbers" and click "Find." All of 1 Cor. 2 will appear on the

screen with most of the words highlighted in blue. Clicking on

any of these will bring up a new screen that will tell you the Greek

word used here, its possible definitions, and the total number of

times it is used in each book of the New Testament (NT). Click on

any of the other NT books (under the title "NAS Verse Count")

and get a display of every verse in that book that uses this Greek

word. To refine your understanding of Paul's use of a word, look

at some of his uses in his other books, such as Romans or

Philippians.

Interpretive Method 4: Study cross-references (cr. rf.). Cross-

references are simply other passages in the Bible that are

somehow related to the study passage. They often prove

incredibly helpful as we seek to understand our passage. You can

find a few cross references in the margins of most Bibles, but you

can find many more by logging onto another helpful website:

net.bible.org. In the top left of the screen under "Display Bible," choose "1 Corinthians," then the chapter you are interested in, and then click "Go." A new screen will appear with the NET Bible translation of the chapter you requested. Click the "XRef" tab at the top of the screen, and this will take you to an extensive list of cross references for every verse in this chapter based on the classic book "The Treasury of Scripture Knowledge." Clicking any of these will bring up the single verse, but you can then click "context" to see the verse amid its surrounding context.

Interpretive Method 5: Look up background info. You can find very helpful insights by looking up confusing names or words in a Bible dictionary or looking up the verses you are studying in a background commentary. One of the best dictionaries is "The New Bible Dictionary" by Wood & Marshall, but you can also find the older "Int'l Standard Bible Dictionary" (ISBE) online for free (net.bible.org/dictionary.php). The "IVP Bible Background Commentary" by Craig Keeneris an excellent example of a verse-by-verse background resource.

Interpretive Method 6: Tackle tough questions step-by-step.

When trying to answer the most challenging questions, follow this four-step process:

(1) LIST ALL THE OPTIONS. Always start by brainstorming every possible answer to your question.

(2) LIST PROS AND CONS FOR EACH OPTION. Seek out all the evidence you can find that either argues for or against an option. This evidence comes from your study of key words, the grammar of the sentence, the context of surrounding verses, the book, cross references to other books, and comparison with your overall understanding of Christian theology.

(3) CHOOSE THE MOST LIKELY OPTION. Look back at your evidence for each option. Typically, evidence from the immediate context is most important, followed closely by evidence from the book. Evidence from other books or from Christian theology does not carry as much weight unless the solution contradicts a clear passage elsewhere or a major tenant of Christian doctrine. In that case, since Scripture never lies and God can not contradict Himself, you know that solution will not work.

(4) DECIDE ON YOUR CERTAINTY LEVEL. Once you have chosen the best solution, step back for a second and humbly gauge how certain you are of its accuracy (90% = I am very sure, this is correct... 60% =this solution is just a bit more likely than the others!) Finally, talk with others and check commentaries or reference books to see what solutions they have chosen and why.

APPLY: How does it work?

Our Bible study is not over until we apply what we have learned to our everyday lives. And lest we underestimate the value of this last step, remember that in God's eyes it is the person who does not just know His Word, but also obeys His Word that truly loves Him (see John 14:21). So how do we apply this passage to our lives? Application involves the following two tasks:

Application Task 1: List potential principles from your passage. A "principle" is simply a fact or command stated or implied in a passage that is practically relevant to our lives. Legitimate principles are not specific to a particular person (e.g. 1 Tim. 5:23 is just for Timothy) nor a particular time (e.g. "do not leave Jerusalem" in Acts 1:4). An example from 1 Cor. 2 would be, "We can find true wisdom by reading God's Word as we rely on His Spirit to help us understand it." It is often helpful when listing principles to consider the following questions:

Is there something to worship or thank God for?

Is there a promise for me to claim or a truth for me to believe?

Is there something I am convicted about that I need to change or begin doing?

Is there something or someone I need to pray for specifically this week?

Is there any relationship I need to work on?

Application Task 2: Choose one principle and create a plan to apply it to your life this week. Once you complete your principle list, prayerfully choose the one principle you most need to work on (do not just choose the easiest to apply!) If you felt deeply convicted about one, that is probably the one God is leading you to apply! Once you have chosen a specific principle, answer these two questions:

What exactly will I do differently this week to apply this principle to my life (be specific)?

Who, other than the Lord, will I ask to help me follow through with this application?

Recommended Resources:

Bible Study Methods:

*The Joy of Discovery by Oletta Wald Helpful, very short booklet on basic inductive Bible study methods.

*Living by the Book by Howard Hendricks Classic medium-length guide to Bible study; a helpful supplement to GBC's Inductive Bible Study notes.

*Greek for the Rest of Us by William D. Mounce Medium length guide that will help those who do not know biblical Greek get the most out of studying the NT; includes detailed discussion of basic Greek syntax along with practical guides to key bible study methods (e.g. Greek word studies, analysis of structural indicators, etc.).

Bible Dictionaries and Word Study Tools:

*The New Bible Dictionary by D. Wood and I. Howard Marshall (3rd edition; 1996) The best single resource for good background articles on key biblical words, places, people, objects, themes, and events.

*Mounce's Complete Expository Dictionary of Old and New Testament Words by William D. Mounce Provides in-depth definitions for most of the Greek and Hebrew words found in the Bible. No Greek or Hebrew knowledge needed.

Bible Commentaries:

*The Bible Knowledge Commentary by J. F. Walvoord and R. B. Zuck (1 vol for OT, 1 for NT) Best single-volume commentary on either testament from a dispensational perspective.

*Expositor's Bible Commentary: Abridged Edition, Two Volume Set by Kenneth L. Barker and John E. Kohlenberger III Excellent two volume commentary on the entire Bible from an evangelical perspective.

*www.soniclight.com Dr. Tom Constable's Expository Notes are free on this site; basically, mini commentaries on every book of the Bible by a Dallas Theological Seminary professor.

Helpful Websites:

*www.biblestudytools.net Free resource for language study – includes Greek text, Strong's numbers, and many English translations; can do full concordance searches; contains some antiquated commentaries.

*www.bible.org NETbible translation as well as articles by many Dallas Theological Seminary professors on a wide variety of resources.

Bible Study Software:

*LOGOS Bible Software 3 – Christian Home Library or Bible Study Library at www.logos.com Very powerful electronic Bible study library; these are both upgradeable base versions (Interlinear Bibles, Greek concordance, New Bible Dictionary, Bible Knowledge Commentary, Ryrie's and Enns' systematic theologies).

(Used with permission from Grace Bible Church, College Station, Texas)

Appendix C

Resources for Police Wives

Websites:

National Alliance for Law Enforcement Support – FB page -

http://nalestough.org

Police Wives of America- FB page –

www.policewivesofamerica.org

Thin Blue Line Foundation –

http://thinbluelinefoundation.org/spouses/

PoliceOne.com

National Police Wives Association- FB page

Badge of Hope Ministries- FB page - http://

www.badgeofhopeministries.com/

Wives on Duty Ministries- FB page

Faith Behind the Badge – FB page

The Police Wife Life- FB page-

http://www.thepolicewifelifeblog.com/

Blue H.E.L.P. – FB page- www.bluehelp.org

Humanizing the Badge- FB page

How to Love Your Cop- FB page- www.how2loveyourcop.com

Billy Graham Evangelistic Association – National Law

Enforcement Retreats- https://billygraham.org/what-we-

do/evangelism-outreach/rapid-response-team/law-enforcement-

ministry/

Focus on the Family-

https://www.focusonthefamily.com/media/daily-

broadcast/help-for-families-of-first-responders-pt1

Books:

The Proverbs 31 Police Wife

by Leah Everly

The Peacemaker's Wife: A Journal for Reflection &

Encouragement for Your Life as a Police Wife

by Rebecca Lynn

Bullets in the Washing Machine

by Melissa Littles

Cuffs & Coffee: A Devotional for Wives of Law Enforcement

by Allison P. Uribe

The Crazy Lives of Police Wives

by Carolyn Whiting and Carolyn LaRoche

Wives Behind the Blue

by Monica Amor

Under Fire: Marriage Through the Eyes of a Cop's Wife

by Kristi M. Neace

I Love a Cop, Third Edition: What Police Families Need to Know

by Ellen Kirschman

Bulletproof Marriage: A 90-Day Devotional

by Adam Davis and Lt. Col. David Grossman

Because I'm Suitable: The Journey of a Wife on Duty

by Allison Uribe

Emotional Survival for Law Enforcement: A Guide for Officers and Their Families

by Kevin M Gilmartin

Melissa Humes is the wife of a College Station, Texas police officer. They have been married 24 years and have 8 daughters; ages 22 to 8 years old. She has taught all her children at home and has led numerous Bible studies over the years. She and her husband attend Grace Bible Church in College Station, Texas.

Made in the USA
Monee, IL
16 October 2022

15997001R00069